I have ten cents.
What can I get?

          1

Can I get the hen?
Yes! You bet I can!

2

Now I have six cents!
What can I get?

Can I get the jet?
Yes! You bet I can!

I have just three cents left.
What can I get?

Can I get the red pen?
Yes! You bet I can!

6

I have a hen, a jet, and a pen.

I still have two cents left!
What else can I get?

8